A Little Book
About

Me and my
Grandma

illustrated by Jedda Robaard

little bee books

This is a book to fill in and share with your grandma.
You may need some help to complete it—that's what grandmas are for!
You can use the pouch in the back of the book to store photographs,
postcards, birthday cards, and anything else that is special to you and your grandma.
Write a special message for your grandma on the card provided.

little bee books
An imprint of Bonnier Publishing Group
853 Broadway, New York, New York 10003
Text copyright © 2012 by The Five Mile Press
Illustrations copyright © 2012 by Jedda Robaard
This little bee books edition, 2016.
Manufactured in China LEO 1115
First Edition 2 4 6 8 10 9 7 5 3 1
ISBN 978-1-4998-0251-1

littlebeebooks.com
bonnierpublishing.com

This is my
grandma
and me.

↖ Draw or attach a photo of you and your grandma here.

Grandma was born in
a place called

....

Now she lives in
a place called

....

I live in a
place called

....

Mark these places on the map.

My
grandma's
mom

is named

....

She is my great-grandma!

Me

Mom

Siblings

Dad

Grandparents

Grandparents

Great-grandparents

Great-grandparents

My Family

Fill in your
family tree.

When grandma was little,

her favorite games were:

....

....

Grandma and I love playing games.
Our favorite game is:

....

When grandma was young,

she had a pet ....

named ....

I have a pet ....

named ....

Our pets never met, but here is
a picture of both of them!

Draw a picture ↗
of your pets here.

When grandma was little,

she wanted to be a ....

When I grow up, I want to be a ....

Here is a picture of my grandma dressed as a ....

She looks ....

Draw a costume on grandma.

Grandma's favorite
color is

....

My favorite color is

....

Here are some flowers in our favorite colors

Draw
and color
in the
flowers.

When we are
together,
grandma
and I love to eat.

Our favorite foods

Make a list or draw your favorite foods here.

For my birthday,
grandma
likes to make

....

My favorite birthday present from grandma was ....

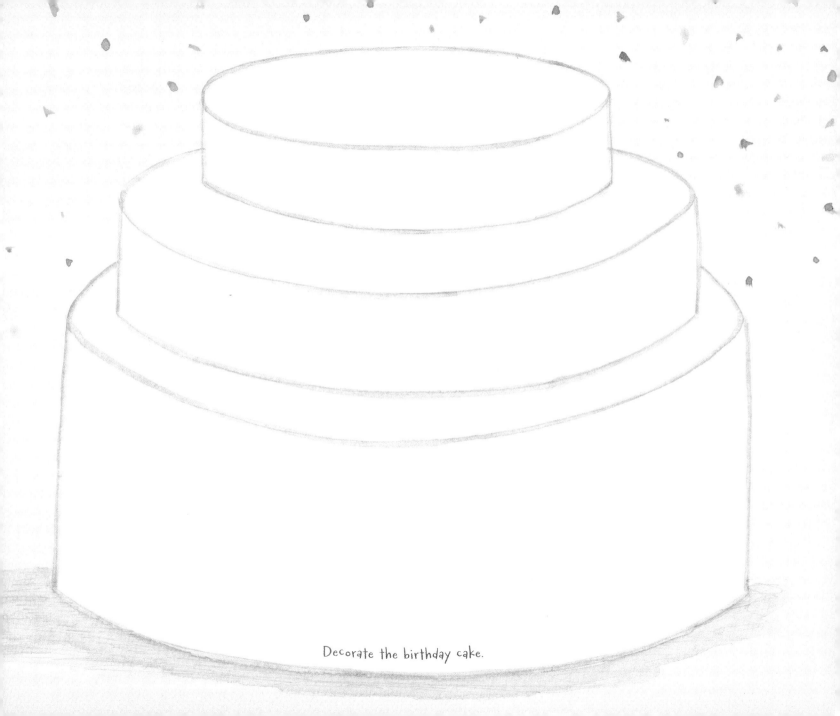

Decorate the birthday cake.

Grandma loves going on vacation.

Her favorite trip was to

....

The best place grandma and
I have been together is

....

Draw or attach a photo of you ↗
and your grandma on vacation.

Grandma's
favorite book
is

My favorite
book is

Grandma's favorite
story to read to me is

I love my grandma.

That's why I've made this special book and card just for her!